D0835363

KEEP
CALM
YOU'RE ONLY

70

summersdale

KEEP CALM YOU'RE ONLY 70

An Hachette UK Company
www.hachette.co.uk

Summersdale Publishers Ltd
Part of Octopus Publishing Group Limited
Carmelite House
50 Victoria Embankment
LONDON
EC4Y 0DZ
UK

www.summersdale.com

Printed and bound in China

ISBN: 978-1-78783-306-7

Substantial discounts on bulk quantities of Summersdale books are available to corporations, professional associations and other organisations. For details contact general enquiries: telephone: +44 (0) 1243 771107 or email: enquiries@summersdale.com.

TO Anne

Happy Birthday

FROM Mary

x x x

BEING 70 IS NO
DIFFERENT FROM BEING
69. IT'S A ROUND
NUMBER, AND THERE'S
SOMETHING ABOUT
ROUNDNESS THAT HAS
ALWAYS APPEALED.

ELIZABETH TAYLOR

THE THREE AGES OF MAN:

YOUTH, MIDDLE AGE AND "MY WORD, YOU DO LOOK WELL".

JUNE WHITFIELD

THE OLD AGE OF AN EAGLE IS BETTER THAN THE YOUTH OF A SPARROW.

PROVERB

THE KEY TO
SUCCESSFUL AGEING
IS TO PAY AS LITTLE
ATTENTION TO IT
AS POSSIBLE.

JUDITH REGAN

OUR BIRTHDAYS ARE
FEATHERS IN THE BROAD
WING OF TIME.

JEAN PAUL RICHTER

I intend to live
forever, or die trying.

GROUCHO MARX

A BIRTHDAY IS JUST THE FIRST DAY OF ANOTHER 365-DAY JOURNEY AROUND THE SUN. ENJOY THE TRIP.

ANONYMOUS

BIRTHDAYS

ARE GOOD FOR YOU.
STATISTICS SHOW THAT
THE PEOPLE WHO HAVE THE
MOST LIVE THE LONGEST.

LARRY LORENZONI

ALL THE WORLD IS A BIRTHDAY CAKE, SO TAKE A PIECE, BUT NOT TOO MUCH.

GEORGE HARRISON

OUR WRINKLES ARE
OUR MEDALS OF THE
PASSAGE OF LIFE. THEY
ARE WHAT WE HAVE
BEEN THROUGH AND
WHO WE WANT TO BE.

LAUREN HUTTON

To be 70 years young
is sometimes far more
cheerful and hopeful
than to be 40 years old.

OLIVER WENDELL HOLMES JR

WHATEVER WITH THE PAST
HAS GONE, THE BEST IS
ALWAYS YET TO COME.

LUCY LARCOM

EVENTUALLY YOU WILL
REACH A POINT WHEN
YOU STOP LYING ABOUT
YOUR AGE AND START
BRAGGING ABOUT IT.

WILL ROGERS

FOR ALL THE
ADVANCES IN MEDICINE,
THERE IS STILL NO CURE FOR
THE COMMON BIRTHDAY.

JOHN GLENN

IF WE COULD BE TWICE YOUNG AND TWICE OLD WE COULD CORRECT ALL OUR MISTAKES.

EURIPIDES

A HUG IS THE PERFECT GIFT: ONE SIZE FITS ALL, AND NOBODY MINDS IF YOU EXCHANGE IT.

ANONYMOUS

I'M HAPPY TO REPORT
THAT MY INNER CHILD
IS STILL AGELESS.

JAMES BROUGHTON

Youth is the gift of
nature, but age is
a work of art.

GARSON KANIN

A DIPLOMAT
IS A MAN WHO
ALWAYS REMEMBERS
A WOMAN'S
BIRTHDAY BUT NEVER
REMEMBERS HER AGE.

ROBERT FROST

TO BE
70 YEARS OLD

IS LIKE CLIMBING THE ALPS.
YOU REACH A SNOW-CROWNED
SUMMIT, AND SEE BEHIND
YOU THE DEEP VALLEY
STRETCHING MILES...

HENRY WADSWORTH LONGFELLOW

LET US CELEBRATE THE OCCASION WITH WINE AND SWEET WORDS.

TITUS MACCIUS PLAUTUS

YOU KNOW YOU ARE
GETTING OLD WHEN
THE CANDLES COST
MORE THAN THE CAKE.

BOB HOPE

I have everything I had
20 years ago, only it's
all a little bit lower.

GYPSY ROSE LEE

A FRIEND NEVER DEFENDS
A HUSBAND WHO GETS
HIS WIFE AN ELECTRIC
SKILLET FOR HER BIRTHDAY.

ERMA BOMBECK

WHEN I WAS YOUNG
I THOUGHT THAT
MONEY WAS THE MOST
IMPORTANT THING IN
LIFE; NOW THAT I AM
OLD I KNOW THAT IT IS.

OSCAR WILDE

A GIFT

CONSISTS NOT IN
WHAT IS DONE OR GIVEN,
BUT IN THE INTENTION
OF THE GIVER OR DOER.

SENECA

I WILL NEVER GIVE IN TO OLD AGE UNTIL I BECOME OLD. AND I'M NOT OLD YET!

TINA TURNER

WE KNOW WE'RE
GETTING OLD WHEN
THE ONLY THING
WE WANT FOR OUR
BIRTHDAY IS NOT TO
BE REMINDED OF IT.

ANONYMOUS

A COMFORTABLE OLD
AGE IS THE REWARD OF
A WELL-SPENT YOUTH.

MAURICE CHEVALIER

The years teach
much which the
days never know.

RALPH WALDO EMERSON

THE OLDER THE FIDDLE, THE SWEETER THE TUNE.

PROVERB

LAST WEEK

THE CANDLE FACTORY
BURNED DOWN. EVERYONE
JUST STOOD AROUND AND
SANG "HAPPY BIRTHDAY".

STEVEN WRIGHT

AGE IS NOT IMPORTANT UNLESS YOU'RE A CHEESE.

HELEN HAYES

WHY IS A BIRTHDAY CAKE
THE ONLY FOOD YOU
CAN BLOW ON AND SPIT
ON AND EVERYBODY
RUSHES TO GET A PIECE?

BOBBY KELTON

I still have a full deck;
I just shuffle slower now.

ANONYMOUS

FEW PEOPLE KNOW
HOW TO BE OLD.

FRANÇOIS DE LA ROCHEFOUCAULD

ONE OF THE
ADVANTAGES OF BEING
70 IS THAT YOU ONLY
NEED FOUR HOURS'
SLEEP. TRUE, YOU
NEED IT FOUR TIMES
A DAY, BUT STILL.

DENIS NORDEN

I AM GETTING
TO AN AGE WHEN I CAN
ONLY ENJOY THE LAST SPORT
LEFT. IT IS CALLED HUNTING
FOR YOUR SPECTACLES.

EDWARD GREY

AGE IS A MATTER OF FEELING, NOT OF YEARS.

GEORGE WILLIAM CURTIS

OLD AGE IS AN
EXCELLENT TIME
FOR OUTRAGE. MY
GOAL IS TO SAY
OR DO AT LEAST
ONE OUTRAGEOUS
THING EVERY WEEK.

MAGGIE KUHN

YOUTH DISSERVES;
MIDDLE AGE CONSERVES;
OLD AGE PRESERVES.

MARTIN H. FISCHER

Father Time is not
always a hard parent.

CHARLES DICKENS

YOU REALLY HAVEN'T CHANGED IN 70 YEARS. YOUR BODY CHANGES... YOU DON'T CHANGE AT ALL.

DORIS LESSING

THE YEARS BETWEEN

50 AND 70 ARE THE HARDEST.
YOU ARE ALWAYS BEING ASKED
TO DO THINGS, AND YOU ARE
NOT YET DECREPIT ENOUGH
TO TURN THEM DOWN.

T. S. ELIOT

PERHAPS ONE HAS TO BE VERY OLD BEFORE ONE LEARNS TO BE AMUSED RATHER THAN SHOCKED.

PEARL S. BUCK

HOW BEAUTIFULLY
LEAVES GROW OLD.
HOW FULL OF LIGHT
AND COLOUR ARE
THEIR LAST DAYS.

JOHN BURROUGHS

70

I'm growing old;
I delight in the past.

HENRI MATISSE

THE LONGER I LIVE, THE MORE BEAUTIFUL LIFE BECOMES.

FRANK LLOYD WRIGHT

A HEALTHY OLD FELLOW,
WHO IS NOT A FOOL,
IS THE HAPPIEST
CREATURE LIVING.

RICHARD STEELE

AT MY AGE

"GETTING LUCKY" MEANS
FINDING MY CAR IN
THE PARKING LOT.

ANONYMOUS

I CAN STILL ENJOY SEX AT 74. I LIVE AT 75, SO IT'S NO DISTANCE.

BOB MONKHOUSE

ONE OF THE BEST
PARTS OF GROWING
OLDER? YOU CAN
FLIRT ALL YOU
LIKE SINCE YOU'VE
BECOME HARMLESS.

LIZ SMITH

THE MORE YOU PRAISE
AND CELEBRATE YOUR
LIFE, THE MORE THERE IS
IN LIFE TO CELEBRATE.

OPRAH WINFREY

Laughter doesn't
require teeth.

BILL NEWTON

IT'S IMPORTANT TO
HAVE A TWINKLE
IN YOUR WRINKLE.

ANONYMOUS

HOW PEOPLE

KEEP CORRECTING US WHEN
WE ARE YOUNG! THERE IS
ALWAYS SOME BAD HABIT
OR OTHER THEY TELL US WE
OUGHT TO GET OVER. YET
MOST BAD HABITS ARE TOOLS
TO HELP US THROUGH LIFE.

JACK NICKLAUS

WITH MIRTH AND LAUGHTER LET OLD WRINKLES COME.

WILLIAM SHAKESPEARE

I'D HATE TO DIE WITH
A GOOD LIVER, GOOD
KIDNEYS AND A GOOD
BRAIN. WHEN I DIE I
WANT EVERYTHING
TO BE KNACKERED.

HAMISH IMLACH

The whiter my hair becomes, the more ready people are to believe what I say.

BERTRAND RUSSELL

YOU ARE NEVER TOO OLD
TO SET ANOTHER GOAL OR
TO DREAM A NEW DREAM.

LES BROWN

THE AGEING PROCESS
HAS YOU FIRMLY IN ITS
GRASP IF YOU NEVER
GET THE URGE TO
THROW A SNOWBALL.

DOUG LARSON

I ALWAYS MAKE

A POINT OF STARTING THE DAY
AT 6 A.M. WITH CHAMPAGNE.
IT GOES STRAIGHT TO THE
HEART AND CHEERS ONE UP.

JOHN MORTIMER

GIVE ME CHASTITY AND CONTINENCE, BUT NOT YET.

SAINT AUGUSTINE

IF YOU DON'T
LEARN TO LAUGH AT
TROUBLE, YOU WON'T
HAVE ANYTHING TO
LAUGH AT WHEN
YOU'RE OLD.

EDGAR WATSON HOWE

TO ME, OLD AGE IS ALWAYS
15 YEARS OLDER THAN I AM.

BERNARD BARUCH

We are always the
same age inside.

GERTRUDE STEIN

I'M SAVING THAT
ROCKER FOR THE DAY
WHEN I FEEL AS OLD
AS I REALLY AM.

DWIGHT D. EISENHOWER

AGE IS JUST
A NUMBER. IT'S TOTALLY
IRRELEVANT UNLESS, OF
COURSE, YOU HAPPEN TO
BE A BOTTLE OF WINE.

JOAN COLLINS

MOST GRANDMAS HAVE A TOUCH OF THE SCALLYWAG.

HELEN THOMSON

GRANDPARENTS
ARE PARENTS WITH
LOTS OF ICING.

ANONYMOUS

A woman has the right to treat the subject of her age with ambiguity.

HELENA RUBINSTEIN

OLD AGE IS NO
PLACE FOR SISSIES.

BETTE DAVIS

INSIDE EVERY
OLDER PERSON IS A
YOUNGER PERSON –
WONDERING WHAT
THE HELL HAPPENED.

CORA HARVEY ARMSTRONG

THERE ARE PEOPLE

WHOSE WATCH STOPS AT A
CERTAIN HOUR AND WHO
REMAIN PERMANENTLY
AT THAT AGE.

CHARLES AUGUSTIN SAINTE-BEUVE

I DON'T WANT TO RETIRE. I'M NOT THAT GOOD AT CROSSWORD PUZZLES.

NORMAN MAILER

IN THE MIDST OF
WINTER, I FINALLY
LEARNED THAT THERE
WAS IN ME AN
INVINCIBLE SUMMER.

ALBERT CAMUS

I ABSOLUTELY REFUSE
TO REVEAL MY AGE.
WHAT AM I — A CAR?

CYNDI LAUPER

When I was a
boy the Dead Sea
was only sick.

GEORGE BURNS

I'M NOT INTERESTED
IN AGE. PEOPLE WHO
TELL ME THEIR AGE
ARE SILLY. YOU'RE AS
OLD AS YOU FEEL.

ELIZABETH ARDEN

OLD AGE IS LIKE
EVERYTHING ELSE. TO MAKE
A SUCCESS OF IT, YOU'VE
GOT TO START YOUNG.

FRED ASTAIRE

WHEN THEY TELL ME I'M TOO OLD TO DO SOMETHING, I ATTEMPT IT IMMEDIATELY.

PABLO PICASSO

NATURE DOES NOT
EQUALLY DISTRIBUTE
ENERGY. SOME PEOPLE
ARE BORN OLD AND
TIRED WHILE OTHERS ARE
GOING STRONG AT 70.

DOROTHY THOMPSON

The secret of staying young is to live honestly, eat slowly and lie about your age.

LUCILLE BALL

EXPERIENCE IS A
TERRIBLE TEACHER WHO
SENDS HORRIFIC BILLS.

ANONYMOUS

EVERY TIME I THINK
THAT I'M GETTING
OLD, AND GRADUALLY
GOING TO THE
GRAVE, SOMETHING
ELSE HAPPENS.

ELVIS PRESLEY

THE MORE SAND

HAS ESCAPED FROM THE
HOURGLASS OF OUR LIFE,
THE CLEARER WE SHOULD
SEE THROUGH IT.

JEAN PAUL

WE ARE NOT LIMITED BY OUR OLD AGE; WE ARE LIBERATED BY IT.

STU MITTLEMAN

I HAVE A WARM
FEELING AFTER
PLAYING WITH MY
GRANDCHILDREN.
IT'S THE LINIMENT
WORKING.

ANONYMOUS

THEY TOLD ME IF
I GOT OLDER I'D GET
WISER. IN THAT CASE I
MUST BE A GENIUS.

GEORGE BURNS

Age is an
opportunity no less
than youth itself.

HENRY WADSWORTH
LONGFELLOW

OLD AGE IS READY
TO UNDERTAKE TASKS
THAT YOUTH SHIRKED
BECAUSE THEY WOULD
TAKE TOO LONG.

W. SOMERSET MAUGHAM

TO KEEP THE HEART
UNWRINKLED, TO BE
HOPEFUL, KINDLY, CHEERFUL,
REVERENT – THAT IS TO
TRIUMPH OVER OLD AGE.

THOMAS BAILEY ALDRICH

I NEVER DARED BE RADICAL WHEN YOUNG FOR FEAR IT WOULD MAKE ME CONSERVATIVE WHEN OLD.

ROBERT FROST

I'VE REACHED AN
AGE WHEN I CAN'T
USE MY YOUTH AS
AN EXCUSE FOR MY
IGNORANCE ANY MORE.

HELEN-JANET BONELLIE

Don't count your years.
Make your years count.

ANONYMOUS

I HOPE I NEVER GET SO
OLD I GET RELIGIOUS.

INGMAR BERGMAN

THE ELDERLY DON'T
DRIVE THAT BADLY;
THEY'RE JUST THE ONLY
ONES WITH TIME TO
DO THE SPEED LIMIT.

JASON LOVE

TO KNOW HOW
TO GROW OLD IS THE
MASTERWORK OF WISDOM,
AND ONE OF THE MOST
DIFFICULT CHAPTERS IN THE
GREAT ART OF LIVING.

HENRI-FRÉDÉRIC AMIEL

A MAN IS NOT OLD UNTIL HIS REGRETS TAKE THE PLACE OF DREAMS.

JOHN BARRYMORE

NO MAN IS EVER OLD ENOUGH TO KNOW BETTER.

HOLBROOK JACKSON

THERE'S NO FOOL LIKE
AN OLD FOOL... YOU CAN'T
BEAT EXPERIENCE.

JACOB MORTON BRAUDE

I'm too old to do
things by half.

LOU REED

IF NOTHING IS GOING
WELL, CALL YOUR
GRANDMOTHER.

ITALIAN PROVERB

MY GRANDKIDS

BELIEVE I'M THE OLDEST THING
IN THE WORLD. AND AFTER
TWO OR THREE HOURS WITH
THEM, I BELIEVE IT, TOO.

GENE PERRET

FEW THINGS ARE MORE DELIGHTFUL THAN GRANDCHILDREN FIGHTING OVER YOUR LAP.

DOUG LARSON

I WANT TO DIE IN
MY SLEEP LIKE MY
GRANDFATHER –
NOT SCREAMING
AND YELLING LIKE
THE PASSENGERS
IN HIS CAR.

WIL SHRINER

Age merely shows what children we remain.

JOHANN WOLFGANG VON GOETHE

THE TROUBLE WITH RETIREMENT IS THAT YOU NEVER GET A DAY OFF.

ABE LEMONS

THERE WAS NO
RESPECT FOR YOUTH
WHEN I WAS YOUNG,
AND NOW THAT I AM
OLD, THERE IS NO
RESPECT FOR AGE. I
MISSED IT COMING
AND GOING.

J. B. PRIESTLEY

THE PROBLEM

WITH GETTING OLDER IS
YOU STILL REMEMBER HOW
THINGS USED TO BE.

PAUL NEWMAN

YOU ARE ONLY YOUNG ONCE, BUT YOU CAN BE IMMATURE FOR A LIFETIME.

JOHN P. GRIER

I KNOW ONE
SHOULD NEVER SAY
NEVER, BUT I HOPE
I'LL GET OFF THE
BEACH BEFORE THE
TIDE GOES OUT.

TERRY WOGAN ON RETIREMENT

OLD MEN SHOULD HAVE
MORE CARE TO END LIFE
WELL THAN TO LIVE LONG.

ANITA BROOKNER

A man is not
old as long as he is
seeking something.

JEAN ROSTAND

HERE, WITH WHITENED
HAIR... HE DRANK
TO LIFE, TO ALL
IT HAD BEEN... TO
WHAT IT WOULD BE.

SEÁN O'CASEY

THE OLD BEGIN

TO COMPLAIN OF THE
CONDUCT OF THE YOUNG
WHEN THEY THEMSELVES
ARE NO LONGER ABLE TO
SET A BAD EXAMPLE.

FRANÇOIS DE LA ROCHEFOUCAULD

NO MATTER WHAT HAPPENS, I'M LOUD, NOISY, EARTHY AND READY FOR MUCH MORE LIVING.

ELIZABETH TAYLOR

PEOPLE ARE ALWAYS
ASKING ABOUT THE
GOOD OLD DAYS. I SAY,
WHY DON'T YOU SAY
THE GOOD NOW DAYS?

ROBERT M. YOUNG

If I had my life
to live over again, I
would make the same
mistakes, only sooner.

TALLULAH BANKHEAD

BEWARE OF THE
YOUNG DOCTOR AND
THE OLD BARBER.

BENJAMIN FRANKLIN

IF YOU ASSOCIATE
ENOUGH WITH OLDER
PEOPLE WHO ENJOY
THEIR LIVES, YOU
WILL GAIN A SENSE
OF THE POSSIBILITY
FOR A FULL LIFE.

MARGARET MEAD

TIME IS THE COIN

OF YOUR LIFE. IT IS THE ONLY
COIN YOU HAVE, AND ONLY
YOU CAN DETERMINE HOW
IT WILL BE SPENT. BE CAREFUL
LEST YOU LET OTHER PEOPLE
SPEND IT FOR YOU.

CARL SANDBURG

I DON'T FEEL OLD. I DON'T FEEL ANYTHING TILL NOON. THAT'S WHEN IT'S TIME FOR MY NAP.

BOB HOPE

I DON'T DO ALCOHOL ANY MORE — I GET THE SAME EFFECT JUST STANDING UP FAST.

ANONYMOUS

I'M AT AN AGE WHEN
MY BACK GOES OUT
MORE THAN I DO.

PHYLLIS DILLER

Never worry about
your heart till it
stops beating.

E. B. WHITE

ADVANCED OLD
AGE IS WHEN YOU
SIT IN A ROCKING
CHAIR AND CAN'T
GET IT GOING.

ELIAKIM KATZ

NO COWBOY

WAS EVER FASTER ON THE
DRAW THAN A GRANDPARENT
PULLING A BABY PICTURE
OUT OF A WALLET.

ANONYMOUS

I WISH I HAD THE ENERGY THAT MY GRANDCHILDREN HAVE – **IF ONLY FOR SELF-DEFENCE.**

GENE PERRET

THE ONLY REASON
I WOULD TAKE UP
JOGGING IS SO THAT
I COULD HEAR HEAVY
BREATHING AGAIN.

ERMA BOMBECK

When you get to my age life seems little more than one long march to and from the lavatory.

A. C. BENSON

LIFE IS EITHER A DARING ADVENTURE OR NOTHING.

HELEN KELLER

MAY YOU LIVE ALL THE
DAYS OF YOUR LIFE.

JONATHAN SWIFT

THE TROUBLE

WITH ALWAYS TRYING TO
PRESERVE THE HEALTH OF THE
BODY IS THAT IT IS SO DIFFICULT
TO DO WITHOUT DESTROYING
THE HEALTH OF THE MIND.

G. K. CHESTERTON

EVERY WRINKLE IS BUT A NOTCH IN THE QUIET CALENDAR OF A WELL-SPENT LIFE.

CHARLES DICKENS

LIFE EXPECTANCY
WOULD GROW BY
LEAPS AND BOUNDS
IF GREEN VEGETABLES
SMELLED AS GOOD
AS BACON.

DOUG LARSON

A WOMAN'S ALWAYS
YOUNGER THAN A MAN
AT EQUAL YEARS.

ELIZABETH BARRETT BROWNING

Good cheekbones
are the brassiere
of old age.

BARBARA DE PORTAGO

A MARRIED
DAUGHTER WITH
CHILDREN PUTS YOU
IN DANGER OF BEING
CATALOGUED AS
A FIRST EDITION.

ANONYMOUS

THERE'S LOTS
OF PEOPLE
IN THIS WORLD WHO SPEND SO
MUCH TIME WATCHING THEIR
HEALTH THAT THEY HAVEN'T
THE TIME TO ENJOY IT.

JOSH BILLINGS

AFTER THESE TWO, DR DIET AND DR QUIET, DR MERRIMAN IS REQUISITE TO PRESERVE HEALTH.

JAMES HOWELL

AS LONG AS A WOMAN
CAN LOOK TEN YEARS
YOUNGER THAN HER
OWN DAUGHTER, SHE IS
PERFECTLY SATISFIED.

OSCAR WILDE

70

At my age getting a
second doctor's opinion
is kinda like switching
slot machines.

JIMMY CARTER

PASSING THE VODKA BOTTLE AND PLAYING THE GUITAR.

KEITH RICHARDS ON
HOW HE KEEPS FIT

YOU CAN'T STOP THE
AGEING PROCESS.
THERE'S ONLY SO
MUCH OIL YOU CAN
PUT ON YOUR BODY.

ANGIE DICKINSON

AGE SHOULD NOT

HAVE ITS FACE LIFTED, BUT
IT SHOULD RATHER TEACH
THE WORLD TO ADMIRE
WRINKLES AS THE ETCHINGS
OF EXPERIENCE.

RALPH BARTON PERRY

HOW PLEASANT IS THE DAY WHEN WE GIVE UP STRIVING TO BE YOUNG OR SLENDER.

WILLIAM JAMES

I DON'T PLAN
TO GROW OLD
GRACEFULLY: I PLAN
TO HAVE FACELIFTS
UNTIL MY EARS MEET.

RITA RUDNER

TIME MAY BE A GREAT
HEALER, BUT IT'S A
LOUSY BEAUTICIAN.

ANONYMOUS

I'm so wrinkled I can screw my hat on.

PHYLLIS DILLER

DO NOT WORRY
ABOUT AVOIDING
TEMPTATION. AS
YOU GROW OLDER
IT WILL AVOID YOU.

JOEY ADAMS

WHENEVER A MAN'S
FRIENDS BEGIN TO COMPLIMENT
HIM ABOUT LOOKING YOUNG,
HE MAY BE SURE THAT THEY
THINK HE IS GROWING OLD.

WASHINGTON IRVING

OLD AGE IS WHEN A NARROW WAIST AND A BROAD MIND BEGIN TO CHANGE PLACES.

ANONYMOUS

I'M LIKE OLD WINE.
THEY DON'T BRING ME
OUT VERY OFTEN, BUT
I'M WELL PRESERVED.

ROSE KENNEDY

AGE IS A NECESSARY
BUT INSUFFICIENT
REQUIREMENT FOR
GROWING UP.

HENRY CLOUD

If you're interested in finding out more about our books, find us on Facebook at **Summersdale Publishers** and follow us on Twitter at @Summersdale.

www.summersdale.com

Image credits

Cake © FARBAI/Shutterstock.com
Balloons © Kobsoft/Shutterstock.com
Flutes © lilac/Shutterstock.com
Bottle © Janis Abolins/Shutterstock.com
Spectacles © Bojanovic/Shutterstock.com